Retrieval-Augmented Generation (RAG): Empowering Large Language Models (LLMs)

Dr. Ray Islam (Mohammad Rubyet Islam)

Published by Dr. Ray Islam (Mohammad Rubyet Islam), 2023.

RETRIEVAL-AUGMENTED GENERATION (RAG): EMPOWERING LARGE LANGUAGE MODELS (LLMS)

First edition. December 28, 2023.

Copyright © 2023 Dr. Ray Islam (Mohammad Rubyet Islam).

ISBN: 979-8223268512

Written by Dr. Ray Islam (Mohammad Rubyet Islam).

To the one who created me...

Retrieval-Augmented Generation (RAG):

Empowering Large Language Models (LLMs)

Dr. Ray Islam
(Mohammad Rubyet Islam)

Dedicated to my dear ones...

Chapter 1: Introduction

1.1 Retrieval-Augmented Generation (RAG)

W

elcome to the captivating world of Retrieval-Augmented Generation (RAG), a revolutionary approach within the realm of natural language processing (NLP), itself a captivating specialty of artificial intelligence. At the core of RAG lies a powerful alliance between a neural language model and a sophisticated retrieval system. This innovative strategy aims to supercharge language models, like the renowned Generative Pretrained Transformer (GPT), by seamlessly integrating relevant external information.

According to Amazon [1], Foundation models, those intellectual powerhouses trained on vast and diverse datasets, are typically refined in isolation from the ever-evolving world of data. Once their training is complete, they remain oblivious to the information that emerges afterward. While their knowledge is extensive, it often lacks the specificity required for niche tasks. This is where RAG steps in as a beacon of adaptability, bridging the gap by sourcing and incorporating data beyond the model's original boundaries, injecting a dose of tailored relevance into your prompts. Delving deeper into the mechanics and merits of RAG, we gain insights from a seminal paper by Lewis and colleagues [2]. They uncover the potent fusion of parametric and non-parametric memory in hybrid generation models, propelling these models to the forefront of open-domain question answering. Users have expressed a preference for RAG's outputs over those generated by purely parametric models like BART, praising RAG for its factual precision. Moreover, the researchers unravel the mechanics of the retrieval component, affirming its effectiveness and the intriguing possibility of updating the model's knowledge base without the need for retraining—a remarkable leap forward.

As we embark on this journey through our eBook, we will explore the intricate dance between parametric knowledge and the external data fetched by RAG. We will ponder the potential of starting from scratch, perhaps with a denoising goal similar to BART, or maybe another aims altogether. The exploration presented here not only sheds light on the interaction between different types of memory within language models but also paves the way for future discoveries in a multitude of NLP applications.

1.2. Key Elements

Retrieval System: The retrieval component is designed to extract relevant information from a large corpus of documents or a database. This can be achieved through techniques such as keyword matching, semantic search, and other retrieval methods. The purpose of this system is to locate external data that is contextually relevant to the input query or prompt. It plays a critical role in complementing the model's existing knowledge by sourcing additional information.

Neural Language Model: The language model component, akin to those employed in GPT models, generates text based on the input it receives. In the case of RAG, the information retrieved by the retrieval system enriches the input provided to the language model.

Integration of Retrieval and Generation: In RAG, the retrieved information is merged with the original input (pre-trained knowledge) to create a more comprehensive context for the language model. This empowers the model to generate responses or content that not only relies on its pre-trained knowledge but also incorporates specific and up-to-date information from external sources. This integration enhances the relevance and accuracy of the generated content.

Chapter 2: Architecture

2.1. Architecture & Implementation Steps

H ere is an overview of the typical implementation process for RAG:

1. **Pre-Training the Language Model**

First, a large language model such as GPT or BERT is trained on a vast corpus of text data. This model learns to comprehend and generate human-like text.

1. **Building the Retriever**

- Data Indexing: A comprehensive collection of documents, such as Wikipedia articles, scientific papers, and web pages, is indexed. This index serves as the knowledge base for the retriever.
- Retriever Training: The retriever is trained to search the document index and identify the most relevant documents based on a given query. It utilizes algorithms like Dense Passage Retrieval (DPR) or traditional methods like BM25.

1. **Integration of LLM and Retriever**

- Combining LM and Retriever: The retriever is integrated with the language model. When the language model receives a query or prompt, it utilizes the retriever to retrieve relevant external information.
- Query Processing: The language model processes the query and generates a context or sub-query that is passed to the retriever.

1. **Retrieval Process**

- Document Retrieval: The retriever searches the document index to find documents that are relevant to the context or sub-query.
- Document Selection: Based on their relevance scores, a few top

documents are selected.

1. Augmented Generation

- Incorporating Retrieved Information: The language model receives the retrieved documents and incorporates their content into its response generation process.
- Response Generation: The language model generates a response that incorporates both its pre-trained knowledge and the newly retrieved external information. This is how RAG operates.

1. Fine-Tuning for Specific Tasks

The combined RAG system can be fine-tuned for specific tasks such as question answering or fact-checking, enhancing its performance in those areas.

1. Continuous Learning and Updating (Optional)

- Updating the Index: Regularly updating the document index ensures that the retriever can access the most up-to-date information.
- Retraining the Retriever: Periodically retraining the retriever can improve its accuracy and the relevance of document retrieval.

Please note that these steps outline the general process of implementing RAG while retaining the original meaning and purpose.

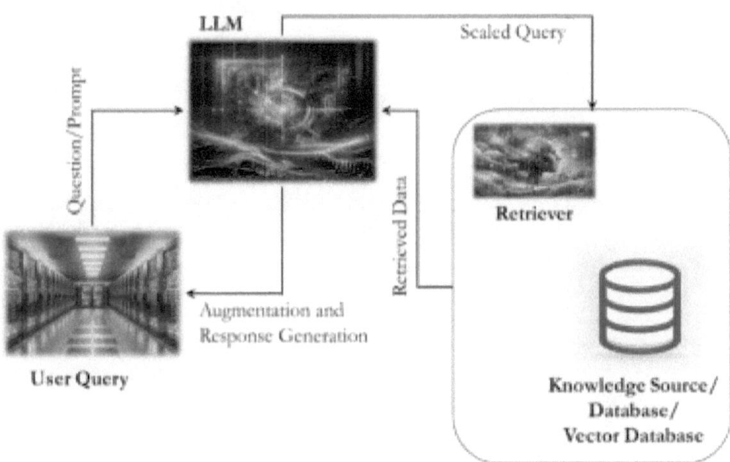

Image: RAG Architecture (Drawn by the Author and symbols are generated by DALL-E)

Chapter 3: Infrastructure

3.1. Infrastructure for RAG

To effectively implement and run Retrieval-Augmented Generation (RAG) models, a well-designed infrastructure is required, comprising several key components, each serving a specific function within the system. Below is an outline of the essential infrastructure:

Computational Resources

- Powerful Processors: Running RAG models, especially for training or processing large datasets, necessitates substantial computational power, often utilizing GPUs (Graphics Processing Units) or TPUs (Tensor Processing Units).

- Ample Memory Capacity: A high memory capacity is crucial for efficiently handling large models and extensive external datasets used for retrieval.

Data Storage

- Document Database: A large and accessible storage system is necessary to house the external dataset or document corpus from which the RAG model retrieves information.

- Scalable Storage Solutions: Cloud storage or distributed file systems are often indispensable, particularly when dealing with vast datasets.

Networking Infrastructure

- High-Speed Networking: Fast network connections are vital for seamless data transfer, especially when the model and data are hosted in different locations or in the cloud.

- Reliable Connectivity: Continuous and reliable network connectivity is essential for real-time applications or when the retrieval system needs to access online data sources.

Software and Frameworks

- Machine Learning Frameworks: TensorFlow, PyTorch, or Hugging Face Transformers are essential frameworks for building and running RAG models.

- Database Management Systems: Effective systems for managing and querying document databases, including traditional relational databases, NoSQL databases, or specialized search and retrieval systems.

Scalability Considerations

- Horizontal Scaling: The ability to scale the infrastructure horizontally by adding more machines is crucial to handle increased loads or larger datasets.

- Load Balancing: Mechanisms for load balancing are necessary in applications with high user traffic to distribute the workload evenly across servers.

Development and Maintenance Tools

- Version Control Systems: Tools like Git enable tracking changes in the model and codebase.

- Continuous Integration/Continuous Deployment (CI/CD) Tools: Automated testing and deployment tools facilitate updates to the RAG model.

- Monitoring and Logging Tools: Tools for tracking the model's performance and swiftly identifying and addressing any issues.

Security Measures

- Data Security: Ensuring the security of stored data, especially when handling sensitive or personal information.

- Model Security: Protecting the model from unauthorized access or tampering.

This infrastructure must be robust and seamlessly integrated to ensure the efficient and reliable performance of RAG models, particularly in commercial or large-scale applications where system demands can be significant. Additionally, Python libraries and packages are often employed in the implementation of RAG models.

3.2. Various Techniques in RAG

Retrieval-Augmented Generation (RAG) models enhance generative models by incorporating external data. However, the integration of the retrieval process can vary. RAG models can be classified into primary categories based on how the retrieval mechanism collaborates with the generative component.

RAG-Token Model:

- This model operates at the token level, where each token generated by the language model's decoder triggers a distinct retrieval query. This unique approach allows for the incorporation of diverse and context-specific information into different parts of the response.

- In RAG-Token, a different document is considered for each target token, enabling the generator to pull content from multiple documents to produce answers. This method involves retrieving the top documents and creating a token distribution from each, resulting in a rich and varied generation process.

RAG-Sequence Model:

- In contrast, RAG-Sequence operates at the sequence level. It uses a single query for the entire input sequence or prompt, and the retrieved data conditions the entire response generation. While not as granular as RAG-Token, this approach offers greater coherence and contextual stability.

- The model treats the retrieved document as a single latent variable, using it to generate the complete sequence. This is achieved by approximating the sequence-to-sequence probability through the top retrieved documents, resulting in a more unified output.

Hybrid Approaches:

- Hybrid models blend elements of both RAG-Token and RAG-

Sequence, sometimes incorporating additional NLP techniques.

- They may use RAG-Sequence for initial generation phases and transition to RAG-Token for parts of the response that require more detail or specificity.

Domain-Specific RAG Models:

- Tailored to specific fields such as legal, medical, or technical, these models utilize domain-centric retrieval databases. This specialization enhances the precision and relevance of the provided information, making them highly effective in their respective areas.

Customized RAG Models:

- Customized models are designed for specific applications, such as chatbots, recommendation systems, or industry-specific Q&A systems.

- These adaptations may involve changes to the retrieval process or the language model to align with the unique requirements of the application.

Each variant of the RAG model brings its own strengths and is chosen based on the specific demands of the application. RAG-Token excels in dynamic and detailed augmentations but is computationally demanding. On the other hand, RAG-Sequence offers stable and coherent responses, albeit with less detail in augmentation. The selection depends on balancing the need for specificity with computational efficiency.

3.3. Tools for RAG

There are various tools and frameworks available for implementing and working with Retrieval-Augmented Generation (RAG) models, primarily in the field of machine learning and natural language processing. Here are some key resources and tools:

Hugging Face Transformers:

- Hugging Face provides an implementation of RAG models in its widely-used Transformers library, a valuable resource in the NLP community.

- It offers pre-built RAG models that can be directly used or fine-tuned on specific datasets.

Dense Passage Retrieval (DPR):

- DPR is a specific component commonly utilized in RAG for efficient document retrieval.

- Tools and resources for DPR, including codebases and pre-trained models, are readily available.

PyTorch and TensorFlow:

- These primary deep learning frameworks are commonly employed for RAG model implementation.

- They provide the necessary infrastructure for building, training, and deploying neural network models.

Elasticsearch:

- Elasticsearch, a powerful open-source search and analytics engine, is well-suited for creating the document retrieval component of RAG systems.

- It particularly excels in scalable search applications.

FAISS (Facebook AI Similarity Search):

- Developed by Facebook AI, FAISS is a library utilized for efficient similarity search and clustering of dense vectors, which proves useful for retrieving relevant documents in RAG.

Apache Solr:

- Apache Solr, an open-source search platform, can manage the document database in RAG systems.

- Solr is renowned for its scalability and performance in search operations.

BERT and Other Transformer Models:

- Pre-trained models like BERT, RoBERTa, and GPT can be integrated into RAG systems for the language generation component.

- These models are accessible through libraries such as Hugging Face Transformers.

Datasets and Benchmarking Tools:

- Datasets like Natural Questions, SQuAD (Stanford Question Answering Dataset), and MS MARCO (Microsoft Machine Reading Comprehension) are valuable resources for training and evaluating RAG models.

- Benchmarking tools aid in assessing the performance of RAG models across various scenarios.

Cloud Platforms:

- Cloud services from providers like AWS, Google Cloud, and Azure offer the necessary computational resources and storage solutions for developing and deploying RAG models.

Jupyter Notebooks:

- Jupyter Notebooks are widely used for experimentation and prototyping, allowing for interactive coding that proves helpful in developing and testing RAG models.

These tools, coupled with appropriate machine learning expertise, facilitate the development and deployment of sophisticated RAG models tailored to specific applications and use cases.

3.4. RAG Users

Retrieval-Augmented Generation (RAG) models are widely used in the field of artificial intelligence, particularly in natural language processing. They find applications in various entities and serve multiple purposes. Here are some key users and applications:

Tech Companies and Research Labs

Major organizations like OpenAI, Google, Facebook AI Research, and others employ RAG models to advance NLP capabilities and research. These models are integrated into their products to enhance language understanding and generation.

Academic and Research Institutions

Universities and research institutions utilize RAG models for academic research in computational linguistics, information retrieval, and AI. They actively contribute to the development and improvement of these models through research projects and publications.

Chatbot and Virtual Assistant Developers

Sophisticated chatbots and virtual assistants rely on RAG models to provide accurate, informative, and contextually relevant responses. These models are particularly valuable when chatbots need to access a vast amount of external information.

Search Engines and Information Retrieval Systems

Companies involved in search technologies leverage RAG models to enhance the relevance and quality of search results, especially for complex queries.

Content Creation and Recommendation Platforms

Platforms that generate or recommend content, such as news aggregators or social media platforms, utilize RAG models to enhance the relevance and personalization of the content they provide to users.

Customer Support Services

Customer support systems, including those with automated responses, can leverage RAG models to provide precise and detailed answers to customer inquiries.

Business Intelligence and Data Analysis

RAG models are employed in business intelligence to generate valuable insights from large volumes of text data, such as market research reports or customer feedback.

Language Translation Services

In the field of machine translation, RAG models play a crucial role in providing contextually enriched translations by retrieving relevant information in both the source and target languages.

The use of RAG models is steadily increasing as organizations realize the benefits of combining sophisticated language generation with dynamic information retrieval. This trend is particularly prominent in applications requiring real-time access to diverse and extensive information sources.

3.5. Common Python Libraries

To utilize Retrieval-Augmented Generation (RAG) models in Python, there are several libraries and packages available. These resources offer the necessary tools for implementing, training, and deploying RAG models. Let's explore some of the key Python libraries and packages:

Hugging Face Transformers

This comprehensive library provides a wide range of pre-trained models, including RAG models. It offers user-friendly interfaces for both the retrieval and generation components of RAG.

PyTorch

As a popular deep learning framework, PyTorch serves as a reliable foundation for training and deploying RAG models. Its flexibility and intuitive interface make it ideal for custom model development.

TensorFlow

Another widely-used deep learning framework suitable for RAG models. TensorFlow is renowned for its scalability and is well-suited for deploying models in production environments.

FAISS (Facebook AI Similarity Search)

Developed by Facebook AI, FAISS is a library that excels in efficient similarity search and dense vector clustering, making it valuable for the retrieval part of RAG.

Elasticsearch

A distributed, RESTful search and analytics engine that effectively manages the document database for the retrieval component of RAG.

Scikit-learn

A Python machine learning library that facilitates data pre-processing and complements the RAG model by supporting traditional machine learning tasks.

Pandas and NumPy

These essential libraries are indispensable for data manipulation and numerical computations. They are instrumental in handling datasets and performing data preprocessing for RAG models.

NLTK (Natural Language Toolkit) or SpaCy

Both libraries provide valuable tools for natural language processing tasks such as tokenization, part-of-speech tagging, and named entity recognition. These capabilities greatly assist in processing inputs for RAG models.

Dense Passage Retrieval (DPR)

If utilizing DPR for the retrieval component, specific libraries and tools dedicated to DPR will be necessary. These may include implementations from Hugging Face or custom codebases.

Flask or FastAPI

For deploying RAG models as web services or APIs, Flask or FastAPI can be leveraged to create server endpoints.

These libraries and packages offer a comprehensive toolkit for working with RAG models in Python, covering data processing, model training, deployment, and integration into larger systems.

Chapter 4: Retrieval Systems in RAG

4.1. Retrieval Systems

The retrieval system in Retrieval-Augmented Generation (RAG) is a crucial component that sets RAG apart from traditional language models. This system plays a vital role in sourcing external information to enhance the model's built-in knowledge.

Function

The primary function of the retrieval system in RAG is to search and fetch relevant documents or information snippets from a large dataset or knowledge base. This external data source could be a collection of text documents, a database, or a structured knowledge graph. According to Microsoft [4], choosing the right information retrieval system is crucial as it determines the inputs to the LLM. The information retrieval system should provide:

- Effective indexing strategies that load and refresh at scale, meeting your content frequency requirements.
- Query capabilities and relevance tuning. The system should return relevant results in the necessary short-form formats for LLM inputs.
- Security, global reach, and reliability for both data and operations.
- Seamless integration with LLMs.

Mechanism

The retrieval process typically begins with analyzing the input query or text. The system then searches its external data source for contextually relevant content. This can involve keyword matching, semantic search techniques, or more advanced query understanding methods that go beyond simple word matching.

Integration with Language Models

The retrieved information is integrated with the input to provide a comprehensive context for the language model. This enriched context allows the language model to generate responses or content that combine its pre-trained knowledge with the specific details from the retrieved data.

Types of Retrieval Systems

Retrieval systems can vary in complexity and approach. Some use simple keyword-based search algorithms, while others employ advanced techniques like vector space models, where queries and documents are represented as vectors in a high-dimensional space. The choice of retrieval system often depends on the specific task requirements and the nature of the data source.

Importance in RAG

In the context of RAG, the retrieval system is essential for expanding the capabilities of the language model. By providing access to a wide range of external information, it enables the model to generate responses that are not only contextually relevant but also informed by the latest or most specific data available.

Challenges and Considerations

The effectiveness of a retrieval system in RAG depends on factors such as the quality and scope of the data source, the accuracy of the retrieval algorithms, and the seamless integration of retrieved data with the language model's outputs. Ensuring relevance, avoiding information overload, and maintaining the coherence of the generated text are key challenges.

4.2 Mechanism of Retrieval System

The retrieval system in Retrieval-Augmented Generation (RAG) models encompasses a complex and integral process. It empowers these models to access and utilize external information, enhancing their ability to generate responses. By incorporating this retrieval mechanism, RAG models can produce contextually relevant and information-enriched responses, making them highly effective for tasks like question answering, content creation, and information synthesis. The mechanism involves several key steps:

Query Formulation

The query formulation process is crucial for ensuring that the retrieval system in RAG models identifies relevant and contextually appropriate information. This enhances the overall effectiveness and accuracy of the model's outputs. When an input, such as a question or prompt, is received by the RAG model, the initial step is to formulate a query that retrieves relevant information. This involves leveraging the input text and employing additional processing techniques, such as extracting key phrases or entities. Query formulation plays a critical role in connecting the user's input with the retrieval process. Here's an overview of how it typically works:

1. Receiving the Input: The process begins with the user's input, which can be a question, statement, or any text prompt. This input serves as the foundation for formulating a query.

1. Understanding the Input: The RAG model analyzes the input to comprehend its context and intent. This involves utilizing natural language processing techniques to parse sentence structure, identify key phrases or entities, and grasp the semantics of the input.

1. Extracting Query Terms: Based on the understanding of the input, the model identifies key terms or phrases that are likely to yield relevant information during the search. This step is crucial for narrowing down the search to pertinent documents.

1. Enhancing the Query: In certain cases, the RAG model augments the extracted terms with additional keywords or phrases to improve retrieval results. This augmentation can involve utilizing synonyms, related concepts, or inferred information based on the input's context.

1. Transforming into a Searchable Query: The extracted and potentially enhanced terms are then transformed into a format suitable for querying the document database. This transformation might involve formatting the query to align with the indexing and search capabilities of the database.

1. Optimizing for Retrieval Method: The query is tailored to fit the specific retrieval method employed. For instance, if the system utilizes dense vector retrieval like Dense Passage Retrieval (DPR), the query may be converted into a vector representation. Similarly, for keyword-based searches, the query would be structured to maximize keyword relevance.

1. Ready for Retrieval: Finally, the formulated query is used to search the document database, retrieving information that will later be integrated into the language model for generating responses.

Search and Retrieve in the Document Database

The formulated query is then utilized to search a comprehensive database of documents. This extensive repository encompasses a diverse range of texts, including Wikipedia articles, books, scientific papers, and other carefully curated sources of information. The objective is to identify relevant documents or text passages that align with the query.

Retrieval Techniques: The retrieval process employs various methods:

- *Keyword Matching*: The simplest approach, which retrieves documents containing the query's keywords.

- *Semantic Search*: More advanced techniques leverage semantic understanding to identify documents that are conceptually related to the query, not just limited to exact word matches. This can involve sophisticated methods like Latent Semantic

Analysis (LSA) or neural network-based embeddings.

- *Dense Passage Retrieval (DPR)*: A widely used method in RAG, DPR utilizes deep learning to encode both the query and the documents into dense vectors within a high-dimensional space. The relevance of a document to a query is then determined based on the proximity of their vectors.

Ranking and Selection

The retrieved documents are ranked based on their relevance to the query. This ranking can rely on traditional information retrieval metrics such as TF-IDF (Term Frequency-Inverse Document Frequency) or employ more sophisticated neural scoring functions. The top-ranked documents or passages are selected for use in the subsequent generation phase.

Integration with the Language Model

The selected documents are seamlessly integrated into the language model component of RAG. This model, trained to generate text resembling human-like responses, utilizes the information from these documents to augment its knowledge. The integration process effectively synthesizes information from both its pre-trained knowledge and the retrieved documents. (This corresponds to the language model section, such as Chat GPT)

Response Generation

Finally, the language model produces a response. This generated response is shaped by the context of the input query, the model's existing knowledge, and significantly, the information derived from the retrieved documents.

4.3. Is Vectorization Useful?

Vectorization is indeed crucial in the retrieval aspect of Retrieval-Augmented Generation (RAG) models, particularly when sourcing information from vast document collections. It facilitates a streamlined and efficient mechanism for searching and pinpointing pertinent data within expansive datasets. Such a process markedly bolsters the language model's proficiency in crafting responses that are not only contextually pertinent but also enriched by targeted external data. Within RAG models, the retrieval mechanism is tasked with identifying the most applicable documents or snippets of information corresponding to a query, which is achieved through a series of vectorization steps:

Vector Representation of Text

Both the query (input text) and the database documents are transformed into vector representations. This transformation is crucial for efficient and effective similarity comparisons.

Utilization of Pre-Trained Embeddings

Pre-trained embeddings such as BERT, RoBERTa, or other transformer-based models are commonly used to create these vector representations. These embeddings capture the semantic meanings of words and phrases, going beyond simple keyword matching.

Dense Vector Space Models

Techniques like Dense Passage Retrieval (DPR) employ deep learning to encode queries and documents into dense vectors. In this high-dimensional vector space, the semantic similarity between the query and documents can be computed more effectively compared to traditional sparse vector methods like TF-IDF.

Similarity Measurement

Once in vector form, the similarity between the query vector and document vectors is measured using metrics like cosine similarity. This step is crucial for identifying and retrieving the most relevant documents for a given query.

Ranking and Retrieval

Based on their similarity scores, the documents are ranked, and the top documents are retrieved to enhance the generation process in the RAG model.

4.4. Input Comprehension Algorithms in Retrieval

In Retrieval-Augmented Generation (RAG) models, various algorithms and techniques are employed to interpret the input text for the retrieval process. These algorithms aim to analyze and extract meaningful information from the input text, which is then utilized to find relevant external data. Working in harmony, these algorithms and techniques facilitate the processing and comprehension of the input text, enabling the RAG model to generate effective queries for retrieving pertinent information from external sources. This process is crucial for the RAG system to enhance its language generation capabilities by incorporating precise and contextually appropriate external data. Key methods involved include:

Natural Language Processing (NLP) Techniques

- Tokenization: Breaking down the input text into individual tokens such as words, phrases, and symbols.

- Part-of-Speech Tagging: Identifying the parts of speech (nouns, verbs, adjectives, etc.) in the text.

- Named Entity Recognition (NER): Detecting and classifying named entities like people's names, organization names, and locations mentioned in the text.

- Dependency Parsing: Analyzing the grammatical structure of sentences to comprehend the relationships between words.

Semantic Analysis

- Word Embeddings: Utilizing pre-trained models like word2vec or GloVe to convert words into vector representations that capture their meanings.

- Contextual Embeddings: Leveraging models such as BERT or GPT to understand the context of words in sentences, which is crucial for disambiguating meanings and capturing subtle nuances.

Information Retrieval Algorithms

- TF-IDF (Term Frequency-Inverse Document Frequency): A statistical measure used to evaluate the importance of a word to a document in a collection or corpus.

- BM25: An advanced ranking function employed by search engines to estimate the relevance of documents to a given search query.

Dense Retrieval Techniques

- **Dense Passage Retrieval (DPR)**: This technique involves generating dense vector representations for both the query and the passages in the database. These vectors are then used to identify the most relevant passages.

- **Embedding-Based Retrieval**: This approach utilizes neural network models to create embeddings of the input query. These embeddings are then matched with embeddings of documents or passages.

Query Expansion and Refinement

- Synonym Expansion: This method expands the query by incorporating synonyms or related terms. This helps to capture a broader range of relevant documents.

- Query Rewriting: This strategy involves modifying the query based on an understanding of the user's intent. By doing so, retrieval effectiveness can be improved.

Machine Learning Models for Query Understanding
Supervised Learning Models

These models are trained on annotated datasets to classify, cluster, or predict aspects of the query. The choice of model depends on the specific task requirements, query complexity, and available training data.

- Support Vector Machines (SVMs): SVMs are effective in classifying queries into different types or intents.

- Decision Trees: Useful for hierarchical decision-making processes in query understanding. They can break down a query into its constituent parts based on specific features.

- Random Forests: An ensemble of decision trees that offer robustness and accuracy, especially in handling diverse and complex queries.

- Gradient Boosting Machines: Models like XGBoost, LightGBM, and CatBoost are powerful for classification and regression tasks. They excel in extracting nuanced features from queries.

- Neural Networks:
    - Feedforward Neural Networks: Basic form of neural networks used for straightforward query classification tasks.
    - Convolutional Neural Networks (CNNs): Originally designed for image processing, they can be adapted for text to identify patterns in queries.
    - Recurrent Neural Networks (RNNs): Particularly effective for sequential data like text. Models like LSTM (Long Short-Term Memory) or GRU (Gated Recurrent Units) are used for queries that require understanding context over longer sequences.

- Logistic Regression: A fundamental classification algorithm often used for binary classification tasks, such as determining the type or category of a query.

- K-Nearest Neighbors (KNN): Used for classification by finding the most similar queries in the training dataset. This can be useful in understanding and categorizing user queries based on historical data.

- Naive Bayes Classifier: A probabilistic classifier particularly effective in text classification. It is useful for categorizing queries based on word frequencies and probabilities.

Deep Learning Architectures

DL Architectures encompass a variety of neural networks, with a special focus on transformers. These networks enable complex understanding and processing of queries. Let's delve into some key architectures:

- Recurrent Neural Networks (RNNs):

- LSTM (Long Short-Term Memory): LSTMs excel in handling sequences and capturing long-term dependencies in text. They are ideal for contextual query understanding.
- GRU (Gated Recurrent Units): Similar to LSTMs, GRUs are efficient in modeling textual temporal aspects, making them suitable for query analysis.

- Convolutional Neural Networks (CNNs):

Adapted for text, CNNs extract high-level features from queries using convolutional layers. They are valuable for pattern recognition in textual data.

- Transformer Models:

- BERT (Bidirectional Encoder Representations from Transformers): BERT and its variants, like RoBERTa and DistilBERT, are highly effective in understanding context and language nuances. They are widely adopted for complex query understanding.

- GPT (Generative Pretrained Transformer): Although primarily used for generation, GPT models can be fine-tuned for query understanding and classification tasks.

- T5 (Text-to-Text Transfer Transformer): T5 frames NLP tasks as a text-to-text problem, making it versatile for interpreting queries in various formats.

- Attention Mechanisms

Incorporated within transformer models, attention mechanisms enable models to focus on relevant query parts, enhancing understanding and context capture.

- Siamese Networks

Siamese Networks create embedding spaces where similar queries are close together, facilitating efficient retrieval.

- Autoencoders

Autoencoders aid in dimensionality reduction and feature extraction from queries, contributing to the understanding of complex query structures.

- Sequence-to-Sequence Models

These models, consisting of an encoder and a decoder, are valuable for transforming one sequence into another. They find applications in query rewriting or reformulation tasks.

- Pre-trained Language Models

ELMo and ULMFiT are powerful models that leverage pre-training on large text corpora. They excel in understanding diverse linguistic patterns in queries.

These architectures empower deep learning practitioners to tackle the complexities of query analysis and understanding.

Chapter 5: Validation of RAG

41

5.1. Performance Evaluation

E

fficiently measuring the performance of Retrieval-Augmented Generation (RAG) models entails evaluating both the retrieval component's accuracy and the quality of the generated text. This comprehensive assessment considers multiple aspects, such as accuracy, relevance, computational efficiency, and scalability. The following highlights key metrics and methods for measuring RAG model efficiency:

Accuracy and Relevance

- Retrieval Accuracy: Assess how effectively the retrieval component fetches relevant documents or information snippets for a given query, measured through metrics like Precision, Recall, and F1-Score.

- Generation Quality: Evaluate the text's quality generated by the model, commonly measured using metrics like BLEU (Bilingual Evaluation Understudy), ROUGE (Recall-Oriented Understudy for Gisting Evaluation), and METEOR (Metric for Evaluation of Translation with Explicit Ordering).

Response Appropriateness

- Analyze if the generated responses are contextually appropriate and factually correct, often requiring human evaluation or comparison against a ground truth dataset.

Computational Efficiency

- Latency: Measure the time taken to generate a response, critical for real-time applications.

- Resource Utilization: Evaluate the computational resources like CPU, GPU usage, and memory consumption required to run the RAG model.

Scalability

- Test how well the model scales with increasing data volume or query complexity, involving stress-testing the model under high-load conditions.

User Satisfaction (For User-Facing Applications)

- Collect and analyze user feedback to gauge how well the RAG model meets user needs and expectations in practical applications.

Consistency and Coherence

- Evaluate the responses' consistency and coherence, ensuring they are both contextually relevant and logically coherent.

Diversity of Responses

- Measure the diversity in the model's responses to ensure it avoids generating repetitive or overly generic text.

Speed of Retrieval Process

- Specifically assess how quickly the retrieval component can fetch relevant information, directly impacting the overall response time.

Custom Metrics for Specific Applications

- Tailor metrics to evaluate performance aspects unique to specific applications such as chatbots or content creation.

These metrics provide a comprehensive view of RAG model efficiency, covering the effectiveness of the retrieval process, the quality of the generated content, and the practical feasibility of deploying the model in real-world scenarios.

5.2. Performance Validation

Validating the performance of Retrieval-Augmented Generation (RAG) models requires a comprehensive evaluation process that encompasses both the retrieval and generation aspects of the model. Here's how you can validate the performance:

Evaluation of Retrieval Accuracy

Assess the accuracy of the retrieval component by using standard information retrieval metrics such as Precision, Recall, and F1-Score. Compare the retrieved documents or snippets with datasets containing known relevant documents for a set of queries.

Quality Assessment of Generated Responses

Evaluate the linguistic quality of the generated text using NLP metrics like BLEU, ROUGE, and METEOR. Compare the generated responses with reference responses (if available) to measure accuracy and relevance.

Human Evaluation

Conduct user studies or expert reviews to assess the relevance, coherence, and usefulness of the generated responses. This provides insights into subjective aspects such as readability and user satisfaction, which automated metrics might overlook.

A/B Testing

Implement A/B testing to compare the performance of the RAG model against other models or previous versions in practical applications. Analyze user interactions and feedback to understand the real-world effectiveness of the model.

Response Consistency and Coherence

Evaluate the consistency and logical coherence of the responses within the context of the query. This can be done through both automated analysis and human judgment.

Fact-Checking for Factual Accuracy

For models used in knowledge-intensive tasks, cross-reference the information provided in the responses with trusted sources or databases to assess their factual accuracy.

Efficiency Metrics

Measure the latency and response time of the model, which are crucial for real-time applications. Evaluate the computational resource requirements, such as CPU and memory usage, to assess the model's efficiency and scalability.

Stress Testing and Scalability Analysis

Conduct stress tests to evaluate how the model performs under high-load conditions or with large-scale data. This helps understand the scalability and robustness of the model.

Diversity of Responses

Analyze the diversity of the model's responses to ensure that it generates varied and non-repetitive answers.

Customized Metrics for Specific Use Cases

Develop and utilize specialized metrics tailored to the specific requirements and objectives of the use case.

By employing a combination of these methods, you can comprehensively validate the performance of a RAG model, ensuring it meets the desired standards of accuracy, relevance, and efficiency for its intended application.

Chapter 6: Pros and Cons

6.1. Key Advantages

R

etrieval-Augmented Generation significantly enhances the capabilities of Large Language Models by ensuring the freshness of information, improving accuracy, reducing biases, enriching content quality, enhancing contextual understanding, and broadening the scope of application. RAG and Its Impact on Language Model Performance:

1. **Ensuring Timeliness with Up-to-Date Information**: RAG plays a crucial role in enabling Large Language Models (LLMs) to access and incorporate the most current information available. This is especially important for time-sensitive topics, ensuring that the generated content remains not only relevant but also reflects the latest developments and data.

1. **Elevating Response Precision Through Enhanced Accuracy**: By integrating external sources of information, RAG significantly improves the accuracy and level of detail in responses generated by LLMs. This enhancement is particularly noticeable in responses to factual queries, where precision and correctness are of utmost importance.

1. **Combating Inherent Biases with External Data Retrieval**: One of the innovative applications of RAG is its ability to address biases that may exist in the training data of LLMs. By fetching and incorporating information from diverse external sources, RAG introduces a broader perspective that helps reduce bias in the model's outputs.

Delving Deeper into RAG's Functionalities:

1. **Richness in Information**: RAG expands its capabilities by tapping into various external databases and the vast expanse of the internet. This not only enriches the responses with more detailed and accurate information but also ensures the inclusion of specialized knowledge,

which is particularly beneficial for queries requiring up-to-date insights.

1. **Enhanced Contextual Understanding**: The retrieval component of RAG excels at discerning and accessing information specific to the user's query. This ability results in responses that are not only factually correct but also contextually aligned with the user's needs, providing a more personalized and relevant experience.

1. **Synergizing Retrieval with Generative Capabilities**: At its core, RAG combines traditional information retrieval with modern generative models. This combination allows RAG to excel in tasks like question answering and content creation, where it can find relevant information and generate coherent, contextually appropriate text based on the input.

1. **Empowering Complex Query Responses**: RAG enhances the effectiveness of generative models when dealing with intricate queries or those that demand detailed, factual responses. By sourcing information beyond the model's training, RAG broadens the scope and depth of the responses.

1. **Overcoming the Limitations of Pre-Trained Models**: Traditional language models often face the challenge of being confined to the data on which they were trained. RAG addresses this limitation by accessing and integrating additional external information, expanding the model's knowledge base and applicability.

2. **Versatility in Application**: RAG's adaptability extends across a wide range of applications. From enhancing the capabilities of chatbots and search engines to refining content recommendation systems, RAG empowers these platforms to generate content that is not only relevant but also informed and insightful.

6.2. Key Challenges

Retrieval-Augmented Generation (RAG) presents several challenges arising from its complex architecture and operational dynamics. These challenges are crucial to address for the effective implementation and optimization of RAG systems:

Computational Complexity and Resource Intensity

- Complex Architecture: RAG systems combine a retrieval component with a generative language model, resulting in a sophisticated architecture that surpasses traditional models in complexity. Managing this intricacy requires advanced algorithms and system designs.
- Resource Requirements: These systems demand substantial computational resources for both training and execution. The retrieval component often involves querying large databases, while the generative model requires significant processing power, particularly for extensive datasets.
- Scalability Issues: Scaling RAG systems while preserving efficiency and speed poses a challenge. As data volumes expand, maintaining a responsive and accurate system necessitates careful resource allocation.

Dependency on Quality of Retrieved Information

- Relevance and Accuracy: The effectiveness of a RAG system heavily relies on the relevance and accuracy of the retrieved information. If the retrieval component sources poor quality or irrelevant data, it directly affects the quality of the generated output.
- Updating Information: Ensuring the retrieved information remains up-to-date is crucial, particularly for time-sensitive applications. Continuous access to the latest data necessitates a dynamic updating mechanism.

Integration and Synchronization Challenges

- Harmonizing Components: Effectively integrating the retrieval component with the generative model is a complex task. Both components must work in sync, and any misalignment can impact overall performance.

- Latency Issues: The process of retrieving information can introduce latency, affecting the system's response time. Optimizing this aspect without compromising data quality presents a significant challenge.

Data Privacy and Ethical Concerns

- Privacy Issues: Retrieving information from external sources can raise data privacy concerns, especially when handling sensitive or personal data.
- Ethical Considerations: The use of external data sources may involve ethical considerations, such as potential bias in the retrieved information or the use of copyrighted material.

Fine-Tuning and Customization Difficulties

- Adaptation to Specific Domains: Customizing RAG for specific domains or applications can be challenging. It requires fine-tuning the model to accurately understand and process domain-specific terminology and concepts.
- Balancing Retrieval and Generation: Striking the right balance between the retrieval and generative components is crucial. Over-reliance on either can lead to suboptimal results.

6.3. Does RAG Serve as a Fine-Tuning Technique?

Retrieval-Augmented Generation (RAG) is not a conventional method for fine-tuning in machine learning. Rather, RAG is an architecture that combines neural language models with a retrieval system to enhance the generation of responses using external data.

In traditional fine-tuning, a pre-trained model is further trained on specific data to adapt it to a particular task or domain. The model's weights are adjusted to improve its performance on related tasks. For example, fine-tuning a language model on legal documents to enhance its performance in legal question answering. In contrast, RAG dynamically incorporates information retrieved from an external dataset during the generation process. It augments the generation by adding relevant external information at runtime, improving the quality and relevance of the outputs.

However, it's important to note that the components of RAG, such as the language model and retrieval system, can be subject to fine-tuning themselves. For instance, the language model can be fine-tuned on specific data to improve initial understanding and generation, while the retrieval system can be fine-tuned to enhance accuracy and relevance in fetching information. These fine-tuning processes, though separate from the core RAG architecture, contribute to the integration of retrieval and generation rather than model adaptation through further training.

6.4. Rag Vs Fine Tuning

Here's a concise comparison between Retrieval-Augmented Generation (RAG) and Fine-tuning techniques [6]:

Knowledge Updates

RAG: Updates retrieval knowledge base directly, suitable for dynamic data environments, and requires less frequent retraining.

Fine-tuning: Relies on static data, necessitating retraining for updates, less suitable for frequently changing information.

External Knowledge

RAG: Efficiently utilizes external resources, especially with structured/ unstructured databases.

Fine-tuning: Aligns external knowledge from pretraining with large language models but is less effective for dynamic data sources.

Data Processing

RAG: Requires minimal data processing.

Fine-tuning: Depends on high-quality datasets; limitations in datasets can impact performance.

Model Customization

RAG: Focuses on integrating external knowledge but offers less customization in model behavior or style.

Fine-tuning: Allows more control over model behavior, style, and domain knowledge, adaptable to specific needs.

Interpretability

RAG: Offers higher interpretability due to traceability of answers to data sources.

Fine-tuning: Often acts like a black box, making it harder to understand model decisions, resulting in lower interpretability.

Computational Resources

RAG: Requires resources for retrieval strategies and database maintenance.

Fine-tuning: Needs resources for preparing datasets, defining objectives, and computing power for training.

Latency Requirements

RAG: Involves data retrieval, which can increase latency.

Fine-tuning: Typically offers lower latency as it operates without the need for data retrieval post-training.

Reducing Hallucinations

RAG: Less prone to hallucinations due to reliance on retrieved evidence.

Fine-tuning: Can reduce hallucinations with domain-specific training but still vulnerable to them with unfamiliar inputs.

Ethical and Privacy Issues

RAG: Concerns arise from the storage and retrieval of external database texts.

Fine-tuning: Ethical and privacy issues may emerge from sensitive content in training data.

Chapter 7: Conclusion

7.1. Conclusion

A s we conclude this comprehensive exploration of Retrieval-Augmented Generation (RAG), we find ourselves on the brink of a new era in natural language processing and artificial intelligence. RAG, combining neural language models with advanced retrieval systems, has revolutionized our approach to understanding and generating human language.

Throughout this eBook, we have delved deep into the intricacies of RAG, uncovering its power to enhance generative models like GPT with the latest and most relevant external information. Our journey has taken us through various facets of RAG, from understanding its complex architecture to exploring its diverse applications. We have witnessed how RAG bridges the gap between static, foundational models and the dynamic, ever-changing landscape of data and knowledge, making it an invaluable tool across multiple domains.

The insights from leading researchers like Lewis et al. have shed light on the depth and potential of RAG. Their work demonstrates how RAG models, with their unique fusion of parametric and non-parametric memory, are redefining benchmarks in fields like open-domain question answering. RAG's ability to update its knowledge base without extensive retraining marks a significant leap not just in efficiency, but also towards a more adaptive and intelligent form of AI.

Looking ahead, the potential applications of RAG are limitless. Its adaptability positions it as a key candidate for enhancing chatbots, search engines, content recommendation systems, and more. The challenges it presents, such as computational complexity and ensuring the quality of retrieved information, pave the way for further innovation and development. These challenges beckon a future where RAG models are seamlessly integrated, efficient, and versatile.

Retrieval-Augmented Generation stands as a testament to the remarkable advancements in AI and NLP. It embodies the relentless pursuit of knowledge and the aspiration to create technology that not only mimics human intelligence but also enhances it. As this field continues to evolve, we can expect even more sophisticated models seamlessly integrating vast knowledge stores, offering insights and capabilities beyond our current imagination.

In conclusion, RAG is not just a technological marvel of our times; it is a harbinger of the future of AI. It opens up new horizons for how we interact with information, how we learn from it, and how we leverage it to solve complex problems. The journey of RAG is far from over, and its continued evolution will undoubtedly be as exciting and impactful as its inception.

7.2. What's Next?

Future advancements in Retrieval-Augmented Generation (RAG) models in artificial intelligence and natural language processing are expected to focus on several key areas:

Enhanced Integration of Retrieval and Generation

- Further refining the seamless integration of retrieval and generation processes.

- Developing more sophisticated methods to ensure the relevance and accuracy of retrieved information.

Expansion into More Domains

- Customizing RAG models for a wider range of specific domains, such as healthcare, law, finance, and others, to effectively leverage domain-specific knowledge.

Improved Efficiency and Scalability

- Optimizing the computational efficiency of RAG models to handle larger datasets and more complex queries.

- Scaling RAG models for widespread commercial and industrial applications.

Advancements in Contextual Understanding

- Enhancing the model's ability to deeply understand and interpret the context of queries.

- Improving the handling of nuanced and ambiguous queries.

Real-Time Information Retrieval

- Developing capabilities for real-time retrieval of information from dynamically changing databases or the internet.

- Incorporating up-to-date information in response generation, particularly important for news, trends, and current events.

Multimodal RAG Systems

- Expanding beyond text to include other modalities like images, videos, and audio in the retrieval and generation processes.

- Developing multimodal RAG systems for a more comprehensive understanding and response generation.

Interactive Learning and Feedback Integration

- Implementing interactive learning where the model can refine its performance based on user feedback.

- Enabling continuous learning from interactions to improve accuracy and relevance over time.

Ethical and Responsible Use

- Addressing concerns related to bias, misinformation, and ethical use of AI in retrieval-augmented systems.

- Ensuring transparency and accountability in how information is retrieved and utilized.

Cross-Lingual Capabilities

- Enhancing RAG models to work effectively across multiple languages, enabling cross-lingual retrieval and generation.

Collaboration with Human Intelligence

- Developing systems where RAG models collaborate with human expertise, combining AI's efficiency and scalability with human creativity and judgment.

As the field of AI rapidly evolves, RAG models are poised to become more sophisticated, versatile, and integral to various applications, driving the capabilities of AI in understanding and generating human language.

Reference

1. https://docs.aws.amazon.com/sagemaker/latest/dg/jumpstart-foundation-models-customize-rag.html

2. Lewis, P., Perez, E., Piktus, A., Petroni, F., Karpukhin, V., Goyal, N., Küttler, H., Lewis, M., Yih, W.-t., Rocktäschel, T., Riedel, S., & Kiela, D. (2021, April 12). Retrieval-Augmented Generation for Knowledge-Intensive NLP Tasks. Facebook AI Research; University College London; New York University.

3. Gao, Y., Xiong, Y., Gao, X., Jia, K., Pan, J., Bi, Y., Dai, Y., Sun, J., & Wang, H. (2023, December 18). Retrieval-Augmented Generation for Large Language Models: A Survey. Shanghai Research Institute for Intelligent Autonomous Systems, Tongji University; Shanghai Key Laboratory of Data Science, School of Computer Science, Fudan University; College of Design and Innovation, Tongji University.

4. https://learn.microsoft.com/en-us/azure/search/retrieval-augmented-generation-overview

5. https://docs.aws.amazon.com/sagemaker/latest/dg/jumpstart-foundation-models-customize-rag.html

6. Gao, Y., Xiong, Y., Gao, X., Jia, K., Pan, J., Bi, Y., Dai, Y., Sun, J., & Wang, H. (2023, December 18). Retrieval-Augmented Generation for Large Language Models: A Survey. Shanghai Research Institute for Intelligent Autonomous Systems, Tongji University; Shanghai Key Laboratory of Data Science, School of Computer Science, Fudan University; College of Design and Innovation, Tongji University.

7. Lewis, P., Perez, E., Piktus, A., Petroni, F., Karpukhin, V., Goyal, N., Küttler, H., Lewis, M., Yih, W.-t., Rocktäschel, T., Riedel, S., & Kiela, D. (2021, April 12). Retrieval-Augmented Generation for Knowledge-Intensive NLP Tasks. Facebook AI Research; University College London; New York University

Knowledge Share

Medium: https://medium.com/@rayislam
Web Page: https://aces.umd.edu/ray-islam
YouTube Channel: @rayisl5382
Twitter: @DrRay010